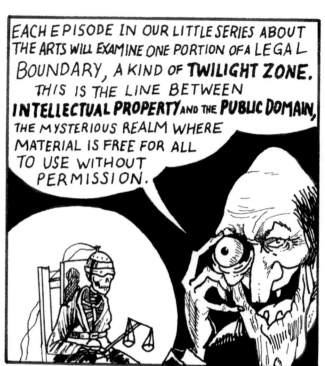

EACH EPISODE IN OUR LITTLE SERIES ABOUT THE ARTS WILL EXAMINE ONE PORTION OF A LEGAL BOUNDARY, A KIND OF **TWILIGHT ZONE.** THIS IS THE LINE BETWEEN **INTELLECTUAL PROPERTY** AND THE **PUBLIC DOMAIN,** THE MYSTERIOUS REALM WHERE MATERIAL IS FREE FOR ALL TO USE WITHOUT PERMISSION.

OUR GUIDES, TWO OBSCURE FIGURES WHO DWELL IN THESE SHADOWS... WHOSE LIVES ARE SPENT IN AN OBSESSIVE QUEST TO CHART THIS LINE, ALMOST AS IF THEY WERE CONDEMNED BY SOME GHASTLY CURSE TO BE THE MAPMAKERS OF **LIMBO.**

CREAK

REVEAL YOURSELVES PLEASE!!

CREAK

CLICK CLACK

CLICK CLACK

CLICK CLACK

CLICK! HI.

HI.

AND WHICH OF THESE ARTS SHALL WE DISCUSS TONIGHT?

WILL IT BE MUSIC?

OR ANIMATION?

WILL IT BE COMIC BOOKS?

NO...

TONIGHT WE ARE LOOKING AT THE PLACE WHERE ART MEETS HISTORY, WHERE REPORTING MEETS THE FEATURE FILM...

TONIGHT WE ARE LOOKING AT... DOCUMENTARY FILM...

HEH HEH HEH

A YOUNG PERSON'S GUIDE TO INTELLECTUAL PROPERTY AND DOCUMENTARY FILMMAKING

SO, TO BEGIN...

DOCUMENTARIES ARE RECORDS OF OUR CULTURE. BUT OUR CULTURE IS FULL OF ARTIFACTS PROTECTED BY INTELLECTUAL PROPERTY RIGHTS --MUSIC, IMAGES, PHOTOGRAPHS.

FILMMAKERS ARE SOMETIMES ASKED TO CLEAR RIGHTS TO THESE CULTURAL FRAGMENTS, EVEN IF THEY APPEAR ONLY INCIDENTALLY.

"CLEARING RIGHTS" IS THE PROCESS OF FINDING THE RIGHTS HOLDER, AND GETTING PERMISSION OR PAYING TO USE MATERIAL.

BUT DOCUMENTARIANS ARE NOT MERELY IN THE POSITION OF DEALING WITH OTHER PEOPLE'S RIGHTS, THEY'RE ALSO IN THE POSITION OF ASSERTING THEIR OWN-- THEY MAY WANT TO RECEIVE PAYMENT, OR PREVENT CERTAIN USES OF THEIR FOOTAGE.

HOW SHOULD THE LAW DRAW LINES BETWEEN FILMMAKERS' NEED TO PORTRAY A CULTURE FULL OF LEGALLY PROTECTED MATERIAL, AND THEIR DESIRE TO PROTECT THEIR OWN WORKS?

LET'S HEAR FROM A FILMMAKER

MEET AKIKO...

8

9

WELL, MANY WORKS PUBLISHED BETWEEN 1923 AND 1977 ARE IN THE PUBLIC DOMAIN BECAUSE THE AUTHORS DID NOT COMPLY WITH NOTICE, RENEWAL OR OTHER FORMALITIES.

BUT TRYING TO TRACK DOWN THIS INFORMATION CAN BE TIME-CONSUMING AND FRUITLESS, SO ARTISTS OFTEN HAVE TO PRESUME THESE WORKS ARE COPYRIGHTED.

DATE OF WORK	PROTECTED FROM
CREATED 1-1-78 OR AFTER *	WHEN THE WORK IS FIXED IN A TANGIBLE MEDIUM OF EXPRESSION
PUBLISHED BEFORE 1923	IN PUBLIC DOMAIN
PUBLISHED FROM 1923 TO 1963	WHEN PUBLISHED WITH NOTICE (WORKS PUBLISHED WITHOUT NOTICE ARE IN THE PUBLIC DOMAIN)
PUBLISHED FROM 1964 TO 1977	WHEN PUBLISHED WITH NOTICE (WORKS PUBLISHED WITHOUT NOTICE ARE IN THE PUBLIC DOMAIN)
CREATED BEFORE 1-1-78 BUT NOT PUBLISHED	1-1-78 (THE EFFECTIVE DATE OF THE 1976 COPYRIGHT ACT)
CREATED BEFORE 1-1-78 BUT PUBLISHED BETWEEN THEN AND 12-31-2002	1-1-78
CREATED BEFORE 1-1-78 AND PUBLISHED AFTER 12-31-2002	1-1-78

*WORKS PUBLISHED WITHOUT NOTICE BETWEEN 1-1-78 AND 3-1-89 RETAINED COPYRIGHT ONLY IF THE OMISSION OF NOTICE WAS CORRECTED.

TERM OF PROTECTION	EXAMPLE
LIFE OF AUTHOR + 70 YEARS (FOR WORKS OF CORPORATE OR ANONYMOUS AUTHORSHIP THE SHORTER OF 95 YEARS FROM PUBLICATION OR 120 YEARS FROM CREATION)	
NONE	
95 YEARS AFTER PUBLICATION DATE; HOWEVER IF COPYRIGHT WAS NOT RENEWED, WORK IS NOW IN PUBLIC DOMAIN	
95 YEARS AFTER PUBLICATION DATE	
LIFE + 70 YEARS	
LIFE + 70 YEARS, OR 12-31-2047, WHICHEVER IS GREATER	
LIFE + 70 YEARS	

* BASED ON PROFESSOR LOLLY GASAWAY'S CHART "WHEN U.S. WORKS PASS INTO THE PUBLIC DOMAIN."

SO THE ONLY WAY I CAN USE COPYRIGHTED WORKS WITHOUT PERMISSION IS TO FIND OUT WHETHER THEY'RE IN THE PUBLIC DOMAIN?

NO, THERE ARE EXCEPTIONS BUILT INTO COPYRIGHT LAW SUCH AS "FAIR USE" - WHICH PERMITS USES FOR CRITICISMS, COMMENTARY AND OTHER PURPOSES...,

FLEETING AND INCIDENTAL USES OF COPYRIGHTED MATERIAL SHOULD USUALLY BE FAIR ... BUT RIGHTS HOLDERS, DISTRIBUTORS AND INSURERS CAN BE CONSERVATIVE ABOUT WHAT'S FAIR, AND REQUIRE CLEARANCES ANYWAY.

SO TO MANY ARTISTS THE QUESTION OF "FAIR USE" CAN SEEM LIKE A GAME OF BLIND MAN'S BLUFF...

OR A SURREALIST GARDEN OF INTELLECTUAL PROPERTY DELIGHTS.

FILMMAKER JON ELSE RAN INTO COPYRIGHT CLEARANCE PROBLEMS WITH "SING FASTER" - HIS DOCUMENTARY ABOUT THE STAGE HANDS' VIEW OF WAGNER'S RING CYCLE.

ELSE DOES GREAT STUFF - I LOVED "OPEN OUTCRY." WHAT KIND OF PROBLEMS?

WELL, HE NEEDED TO CUT AND REPLACE 4½ SECONDS FROM "THE SIMPSONS" THAT WERE ACCIDENTALLY CAPTURED IN ONE OF THE SCENES...

THE SIMPSONS?

STAGEHANDS WERE PLAYING CHECKERS BACKSTAGE WHILE THE OPERA WAS PERFORMED, AND A SMALL TV IN THE BACKGROUND WAS SHOWING "THE SIMPSONS." MATT GROENING DIDN'T OBJECT, BUT FOX DEMANDED $10,000 FOR RIGHTS TO THE 4½ SECONDS!

$10,000

THIS WAS CLEARLY A "FAIR USE," BUT ELSE WAS TOLD FOX WOULD MAKE LITIGATING THE ISSUE DIFFICULT AND COSTLY.

HE TOOK IT OUT - EVEN THOUGH HE THOUGHT IT WAS IMPORTANT FOR THE SCENE.

WOW! SO JUST BECAUSE "THE SIMPSONS" WAS PLAYING IN THE BAR I FILMED, I MIGHT HAVE TO PAY FOR IT?

EVEN IF I DIDN'T USE IT DELIBERATELY, AND WAS JUST TRYING TO CAPTURE "REALITY"?

FAIR USE **SHOULD** MEAN YOU DON'T NEED PERMISSION FOR INCIDENTALLY CAPTURED FRAGMENTS. BUT THE PRACTICE IS OFTEN DIFFERENT.

JON ELSE'S EXPERIENCE IS **NOT** UNIQUE.

MAD HOT Ballroom

DA DA DA DA DA DA DA DA DA DA DUH DA DA DUH

A CELL PHONE HAPPENED TO RING DURING THE FILMING OF MARILYN AGRELO AND AMY SEWELL'S "MAD HOT BALLROOM," A DOCUMENTARY ABOUT NEW YORK CITY KIDS IN A BALLROOM DANCING COMPETITION. THE RING TONE WAS THE "ROCKY" THEME SONG. THIS IS A VERY STRONG CASE FOR FAIR USE.

BUT EMI, WHICH OWNS THE RIGHTS TO THE "ROCKY" SONG, ASKED FOR -- GUESS HOW MUCH?

$10,000!

I DUNNO... HOW MUCH?

IN ANOTHER SCENE, THEY WERE FILMING A FOOSBALL GAME AND ONE OF THE PLAYERS SPONTANEOUSLY YELLED "EVERYBODY DANCE NOW," A LINE FROM THE C&C MUSIC FACTORY HIT.

WARNER CHAPPELL DEMANDED $5000 FOR USE OF THE LINE.

THEY EVENTUALLY GOT A BETTER DEAL ON THE "ROCKY" RING TONE, BUT DECIDED TO CUT THE "DANCE" LINE, EVEN THOUGH IT REALLY FIT THE MOVIE'S THEME.

14

IN "THE FIRST YEAR," A PBS DOCUMENTARY ABOUT LOS ANGELES PUBLIC SCHOOL TEACHERS IN THEIR FIRST YEAR OF TEACHING, LED ZEPPELIN'S "STAIRWAY TO HEAVEN" CAME ON THE RADIO WHILE A TEACHER WAS DRIVING A VAN FULL OF STUDENTS TO AN OUTING.

THE TEACHER TURNED THE SONG UP AND CALLED TO THE CLASS TO LISTEN. THE STUDENTS ROLLED THEIR EYES. IT WASN'T THEIR MUSIC. IT WAS A PIVOTAL MOMENT-- A LIVE GENERATION GAP.

DAVIS GUGGENHEIM, THE FILMMAKER, WAS UNABLE TO CLEAR RIGHTS TO THE SONG AND HAD TO CUT IT OUT...

WHAT ARE MY OPTIONS?

WOW, THAT'S DEMORALIZING. THERE'S A LOT OF MUSIC PLAYING IN THE BACKGROUND OF MY FILM. I DIDN'T CHOOSE TO INCLUDE IT. IT WAS JUST THERE, EVERYWHERE I FILMED.

WELL, YOU COULD ASSERT FAIR USE AND KEEP IT IN THE FILM...

OR TRY TO FIND THE RIGHTS OWNERS AND ASK FOR PERMISSION...

OR OVERDUB IT WITH MUSIC THAT'S IN THE PUBLIC DOMAIN...

HMMM... LET'S SEE...

COULD THE SAX PLAYER IN THE SUBWAY BE PLAYING MOZART INSTEAD OF "I LOVE NEW YORK?"

LEXINGTON AVE

I ♥ NEW YORK

REPLACE THE ROY ORBISON SUNG BY THE STREET MUSICIAN WITH "OH SUSANNAH."

OH PRETTY WOMAN, WALKIN' DOWN THE STREET

AND THE DUELLING HIP HOP SONGS IN TIMES SQUARE WITH JOHN PHILLIP SOUSA...

BOOM THAK

BAM TH

AND REPLACE THE HOT DOG VENDOR'S SINATRA WITH "YES! WE HAVE NO BANANAS."

SABRETT FRANKFURTERS ICE COLD DRINKS

COURT ST

I DID IT MY WAY!!

AKIKO...UM... THAT SONG WAS SET TO GO INTO THE PUBLIC DOMAIN IN 1999, BUT THEN CONGRESS EXTENDED THE TERM FOR ANOTHER 20 YEARS...

?

THE THING IS, THE MUSIC IS AN IMPORTANT PART OF THESE SCENES. REPLACING IT WOULD REALLY DISRUPT THE FILM.

HMMM...

18

NO, THINGS HAVE CHANGED. AND THE LAW ISN'T NECESSARILY DRIVING THIS. FAIR USE ACTUALLY PROTECTS SOME THINGS MORE CLEARLY TODAY.

BUT MANY FACTORS - NEW TECHNOLOGIES ... NEW MARKETS... HAVE CONTRIBUTED TO THE RISE OF A "RIGHTS" CULTURE.

BOB DYLAN DONT LOOK BACK
A FILM BY D.A. PENNEBAKER

UNTIL RECENTLY NO ONE INSISTED ON PAYMENT FOR INCIDENTAL USES...

IF YOU WATCH THE END OF "DONT LOOK BACK," D. A. PENNEBAKER'S 1967 DOCUMENTARY ABOUT DYLAN, YOU'LL SEE THAT THERE AREN'T THE TEN MINUTES OF MUSIC CREDITS THAT YOU MIGHT SEE NOW.

WE USED TO ACCEPT THAT COPYRIGHT DIDN'T GIVE CONTROL OVER EVERY USE.

NOW A LOT OF PEOPLE THINK THE RIGHTS ARE ABSOLUTE!

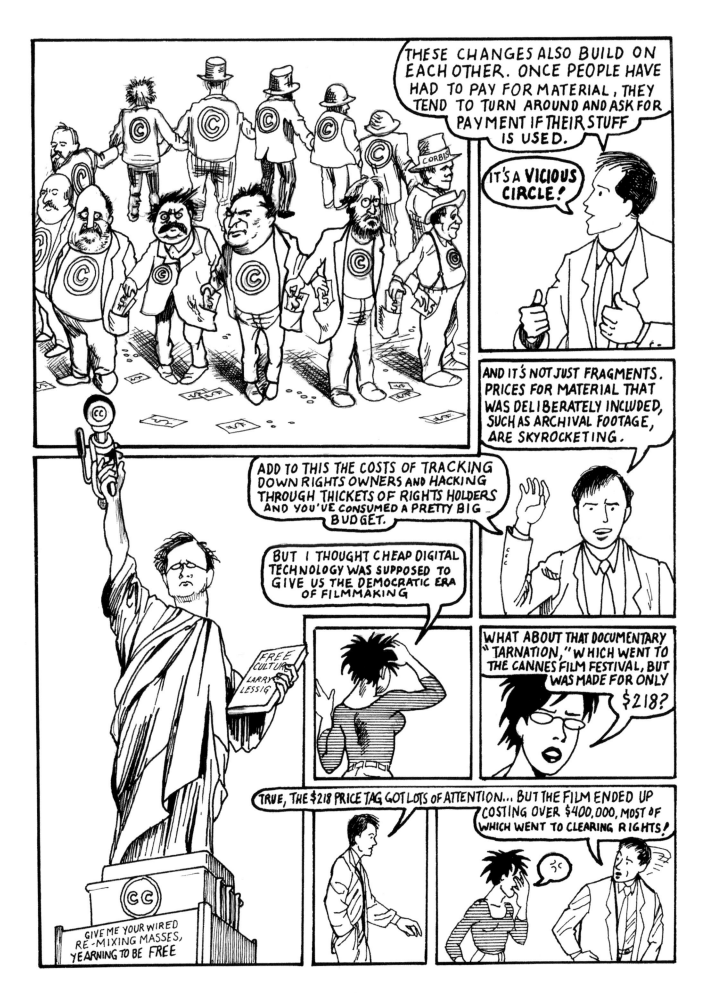

THESE CHANGES ALSO BUILD ON EACH OTHER. ONCE PEOPLE HAVE HAD TO PAY FOR MATERIAL, THEY TEND TO TURN AROUND AND ASK FOR PAYMENT IF THEIR STUFF IS USED.

IT'S A VICIOUS CIRCLE!

AND IT'S NOT JUST FRAGMENTS. PRICES FOR MATERIAL THAT WAS DELIBERATELY INCLUDED, SUCH AS ARCHIVAL FOOTAGE, ARE SKYROCKETING.

ADD TO THIS THE COSTS OF TRACKING DOWN RIGHTS OWNERS AND HACKING THROUGH THICKETS OF RIGHTS HOLDERS AND YOU'VE CONSUMED A PRETTY BIG BUDGET.

BUT I THOUGHT CHEAP DIGITAL TECHNOLOGY WAS SUPPOSED TO GIVE US THE DEMOCRATIC ERA OF FILMMAKING

WHAT ABOUT THAT DOCUMENTARY "TARNATION," WHICH WENT TO THE CANNES FILM FESTIVAL, BUT WAS MADE FOR ONLY $218?

TRUE, THE $218 PRICE TAG GOT LOTS OF ATTENTION... BUT THE FILM ENDED UP COSTING OVER $400,000, MOST OF WHICH WENT TO CLEARING RIGHTS!

FREE CULTURE LARRY LESSIG

GIVE ME YOUR WIRED RE-MIXING MASSES, YEARNING TO BE FREE

21

AND THEN THERE ARE CRITICAL USES...

RELYING ON FAIR USE, ROBERT GREENWALD MADE EXTENSIVE USE OF FOX NEWS CLIPS IN HIS CRITICAL DOCUMENTARY "OUTFOXED."

IN A DISCUSSION OF RACISM IN THE MEDIA, "BOWLING FOR COLUMBINE" USED UNCLEARED FOOTAGE OF NEWS ANCHORS WARNING ABOUT BLACK MALE SUSPECTS.

AND NEITHER USE WAS CHALLENGED!

OUTFOXED:
Rupert Murdoch's War on Journalism

IN FACT, SEVERAL FILMMAKERS' ORGANIZATIONS HAVE JOINTLY PRODUCED A STATEMENT of BEST PRACTICES in FAIR USE TO CLARIFY HOW PROFESSIONAL FILMMAKERS INTERPRET FAIR USE IN DAILY PRACTICE.

FILMMAKERS COULD CHANGE THE "RIGHTS" CULTURE BY LEARNING MORE ABOUT FAIR USE, AND EVEN MAKING SOME COLLECTIVE DECISIONS ABOUT WHAT'S FAIR.

ARTISTS MAY ALSO HAVE SOME AMMUNITION AGAINST UNREASONABLE DENIALS OF FAIR USE.

MATTEL SUED ARTIST TOM FORSYTHE FOR USING TRANSFORMED IMAGES OF BARBIE DOLLS.

THE COURT FOUND THAT THIS WORK WAS A PARODY -- ONE KIND OF FAIR USE.

SO FORSYTHE COULD MAKE IMAGES LIKE...

"MARGARITA BARBIE" OR "LAND OF MILK AND BARBIE!"

IN FACT, A JUDGE IN THIS CASE SAID THAT MATTEL'S LAWSUIT WAS...

"OBJECTIVELY UNREASONABLE AND FRIVOLOUS,"

AND EVEN AWARDED FORSYTHE SUBSTANTIAL ATTORNEYS' FEES.

OK, SO I HAVE CERTAIN RIGHTS UNDER FAIR USE. FOR OTHER CONTENT, IF I CAN MANAGE TO PAY FOR IT, THEN I'M OK, RIGHT?

NOT EXACTLY.

NORMALLY YOU PAY FOR RIGHTS THROUGH A LICENSE, AND THESE LICENSES CAN RUN OUT. YOUR FILM WON'T BE DISTRIBUTED ANY MORE UNLESS YOU ARE WILLING TO PAY TO RENEW THEM.

WHAT? SO IF I GET LICENSES FOR SONGS ON MY SOUNDTRACK, OR PHOTOGRAPHS AND MOVIE CLIPS, THEY CAN EXPIRE?

YES, AND RELATIVELY QUICKLY.

GETTING RIGHTS "IN PERPETUITY" CAN BE EXPENSIVE, AND FILMMAKERS WITH LIMITED FUNDS OFTEN HAVE TO SETTLE FOR SHORT TERM LICENSES. "EYES ON THE PRIZE," THE GREAT CIVIL RIGHTS DOCUMENTARY, DISAPPEARED FROM CIRCULATION BECAUSE THE COST OF RENEWING EXPIRED LICENSES WAS SO HIGH, THE PRODUCERS COULD NOT AFFORD TO PAY THE ESCALATED FEES.

I WAS GOING TO BUY "EYES ON THE PRIZE" AND SHOW IT TO MY KIDS. I CAN'T BELIEVE THAT IT'S OUT OF CIRCULATION --IT'S SUCH AN IMPORTANT RECORD OF HISTORY.

THAT'S DISCOURAGING. IMAGINE TRYING TO TELL THE STORY OF THE CIVIL RIGHTS MOVEMENT IN THE 50s AND 60s WITHOUT THE MUSIC OR FOOTAGE OF THE TIMES.

CAN YOU COPYRIGHT HISTORY?

EYES ON

IRONICALLY, ONE REASON LICENSING FEES ARE GOING UP IS THE INCREASING POPULARITY OF DOCUMENTARIES AND NEW MARKETS FOR ARCHIVAL FOOTAGE. THE MAKERS OF PROFITABLE DOCUMENTARIES ABOUT MARILYN MONROE OR THE NORMANDY LANDINGS MIGHT BE ABLE TO AFFORD HIGHER FEES.

BUT THEN WE TRANSFER THIS "PAY AS YOU GO" ATTITUDE TO LESS COMMERCIALLY ATTRACTIVE FILMS ABOUT PUBLIC SCHOOL REFORM OR MENTAL INSTITUTIONS.

SOMETIMES CULTURAL HEROES GET IN ON THE ACTION. THE MARTIN LUTHER KING, JR. ESTATE HAS AGGRESSIVELY ASSERTED COPYRIGHT OVER DR. KING'S SPEECHES, PHOTOS AND INTERVIEWS. THIS CREATED ENORMOUS OBSTACLES FOR DOCUMENTARIES—SUCH AS ORLANDO BAGWELL'S "CITIZEN KING."

ORLANDO BAGWELL

PBS HOME VIDEO
CITIZEN

ONE CAN UNDERSTAND WANTING TO PROTECT DR. KING.

BUT ANY RULES THAT APPLY TO MARTIN LUTHER KING WILL ALSO APPLY TO DAVID DUKE.

DO WE WANT TO GIVE COPYRIGHT HOLDERS A **VETO** OVER **HISTORY**?

28

Creative Commons is a nonprofit that offers a flexible copyright for creative work.

31

SO, COPYRIGHT GIVES YOU RIGHTS THAT YOU CAN USE TO CONTROL AND GET PAID FOR YOUR WORK.

AT ITS BEST, IT PRODUCES A BRILLIANT DECENTRALIZED SYSTEM OF CREATIVITY!

ARTISTS SOMETIMES THINK THEY WANT TO HAVE AS MUCH COPYRIGHT PROTECTION AS POSSIBLE.

WELL, THIS MAY BE GREAT ON THE **OUTPUT** SIDE; BUT WHAT ABOUT THE **INPUT** SIDE?

IF EVERYTHING IS PROTECTED BY COPYRIGHT, THEN WHERE DO YOU GET YOUR RAW MATERIALS?

BOINK!

NIMMER ON COPYRIGHT

MANS ARE EENS

COPYRIGHT LAW ALSO TRIES TO GIVE ARTISTS ACCESS TO THE RAW MATERIALS THEY NEED TO CREATE IN THE FIRST PLACE.

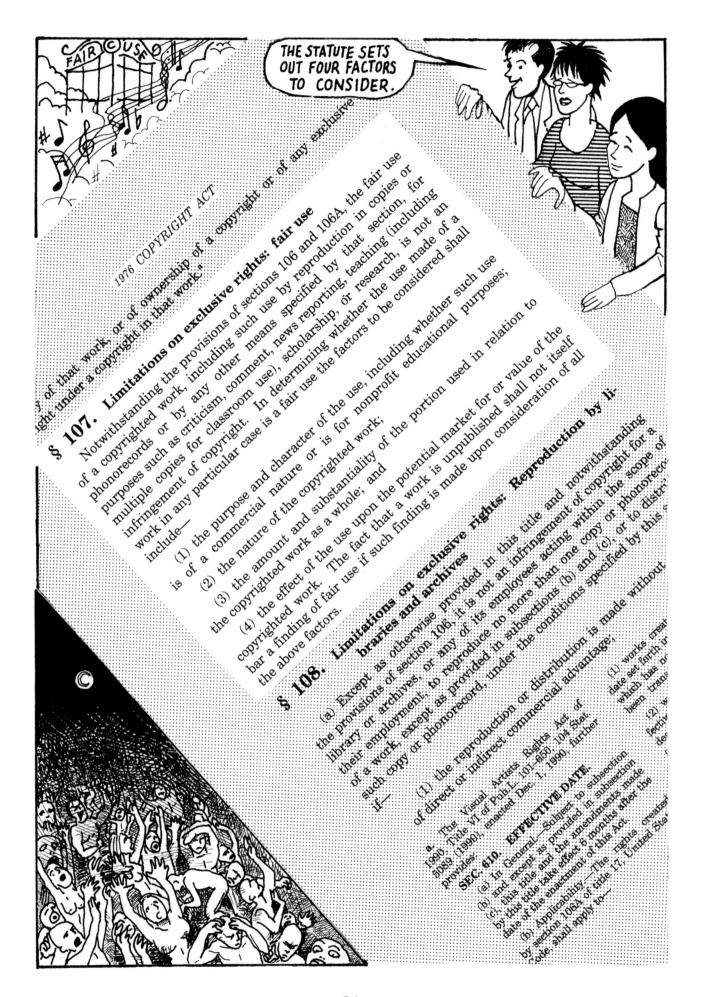

THE STATUTE SETS OUT FOUR FACTORS TO CONSIDER.

1976 COPYRIGHT ACT

...ry of that work, or of ownership of a copyright or of any exclusive right under a copyright in that work.

§ 107. Limitations on exclusive rights: fair use

Notwithstanding the provisions of sections 106 and 106A, the fair use of a copyrighted work, including such use by reproduction in copies or phonorecords or by any other means specified by that section, for purposes such as criticism, comment, news reporting, teaching (including multiple copies for classroom use), scholarship, or research, is not an infringement of copyright. In determining whether the use made of a work in any particular case is a fair use the factors to be considered shall include—

(1) the purpose and character of the use, including whether such use is of a commercial nature or is for nonprofit educational purposes;

(2) the nature of the copyrighted work;

(3) the amount and substantiality of the portion used in relation to the copyrighted work as a whole; and

(4) the effect of the use upon the potential market for or value of the copyrighted work. The fact that a work is unpublished shall not itself bar a finding of fair use if such finding is made upon consideration of all the above factors.

§ 108. Limitations on exclusive rights: Reproduction by libraries and archives

(a) Except as otherwise provided in this title and notwithstanding the provisions of section 106, it is not an infringement of copyright for a library or archives, or any of its employees acting within the scope of their employment, to reproduce no more than one copy or phonorecord of a work, except as provided in subsections (b) and (c), or to distribute such copy or phonorecord, under the conditions specified by this s...

if—

(1) the reproduction or distribution is made without ...of direct or indirect commercial advantage;

a. The Visual Artists Rights Act of 1990, Title VI of Pub.L. 101-650, 104 Stat. 5089 (1990), enacted Dec. 1, 1990, further provides:

SEC. 610. EFFECTIVE DATE.

(a) In General.—Subject to subsection (b) and except as provided in subsection (c), this title and the amendments made by this title take effect 6 months after the date of the enactment of this Act.

(b) Applicability.—The rights created by section 106A of title 17, United States Code, shall apply to—

(1) works crea...
date set forth in... which has n... been trans...

(2) w...
fective...
des...

Sony v. Universal Studios (1984)
Fair use: home videotaping of television shows.

"Time-shifting," or videotaping television shows in order to watch them later, was fair use, said the Supreme Court, even though VCR users were copying the entire programs. One key reason was that the time-shifting was private and non-commercial. That meant that the film companies had to prove market harm. The Court did not believe they had done so.

HERE ARE SOME MAJOR FAIR USE CASES...

LET'S...

...JUMP RIGHT IN!

Campbell v. Acuff-Rose (1994)
Fair use: a rap parody of "Pretty Woman".

The rap group 2 Live Crew made a song called "Pretty Woman" that borrowed the bass riff, much of the tune and some lyrics from Roy Orbison's "Oh, Pretty Woman." 2 Live Crew seemed to have 2 strikes against them. They used a lot of the song, and their use was "commercial." The Supreme Court said that even so, this could be fair use. They saw the song as a parody. It "juxtaposes the romantic musings of a man whose fantasy comes true, with degrading taunts, a bawdy demand for sex, and a sigh of relief from paternal responsibility." Because the song was a parody, 2 Live Crew was also allowed to copy more of it – as effective parodies need to "conjure up the original."

Margaret Mitchell

Suntrust v. Houghton Mifflin (2001)

Fair use: a parody of "Gone with the Wind" from a slave's point of view.

Author Alice Randall wrote a parody of *Gone with the Wind* criticizing its romanticized depiction of slavery and the antebellum South, and in doing so alluded to copyrighted characters and scenes from *Gone with the Wind*.

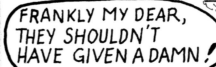

FRANKLY MY DEAR, THEY SHOULDN'T HAVE GIVEN A DAMN!

The Court of Appeals held that this could be fair use: "It is hard to imagine how Randall could have specifically criticized *Gone with the Wind* without depending heavily upon copyrighted elements of that book. A parody is a work that seeks to comment upon or criticize another work by appropriating elements of the original..."

A TIME TO HEAL

With a new introduction about today's America
in crisis written especially for this edition

...BUT THEY ARE!

HE'S NOT A CROOK...

Harper & Row v. Nation Enterprises
(1985)
Not a fair use: scooping President
Ford's memoirs.

The Nation.

Time Magazine agreed to purchase the exclusive right to print a pre-publication excerpt of ex-president Ford's autobiography. Before Time's article came out, the political magazine The Nation got an unauthorized copy of the manuscript. The Nation published its own article, which included 300-400 words from Ford's autobiography about his decision to pardon President Nixon. The Supreme Court said this was not a fair use. Why? The memoirs had not been published yet, and authors have a right to decide whether and when their work will be published. The Court found that The Nation had "effectively arrogated to itself the right of first publication" for the purpose of "scooping" Time's planned article. (Time then canceled the article.) The Court also said that the parts of Ford's book used, though small, were its "heart" – the most powerful and interesting part.

SO HOW DOES ALL THIS APPLY TO ME?

WELL, COURTS HAVE FOUND FAIR USE WHEN DOCUMENTARIES USE SHORT CLIPS IN TRANSFORMATIVE — NEW, DIFFERENT AND VALUABLE — WAYS, INSTEAD OF MERELY "RIPPING OFF" THE COPYRIGHTED MATERIAL.

HERE'S SOME EXAMPLES OF USES THAT WERE FOUND TO BE "FAIR."

ORIGINAL MOTION PICTURE SOUNDTRACKS

INVASION OF THE SAUCER-MEN

IT CONQUERED THE WORLD

MUSIC COMPOSED AND CONDUCTED BY RONALD STEIN

The documentary *Aliens Invade Hollywood* could use 3 clips totaling 48 seconds (1%) from *Invasion of the Saucermen* to show early film portrayals of alien visitations and government cover-ups.

THIS IS A FAIR USE — SO LONG AS YOU DON'T MENTION AREA 51!!!

DON'T WORRY MA'AM, THAT EXCERPT DIDN'T SHOW A REAL UFO... SWAMP GAS FROM A WEATHER BALLOON...,

An A&E biography of Peter Graves could use 20 seconds (less than 1%) of *It Conquered the World*, which starred Graves, to show his modest beginnings in the film business.

THIS MOVIE, SHOULD YOU CHOOSE TO EXCERPT IT, WILL SELF-DESTRUCT IN 20 SECONDS!

41

A TBS biography of Muhammad Ali could use 9-14 clips totaling between 41 seconds and 2 minutes (between .7 and 2.1%) from *When We Were Kings*, a documentary focusing on the "Rumble in the Jungle" fight in Zaire between Ali and George Foreman. (The parties disagreed about the number of clips, so the court used the 9-14 range.)

The Definitive Elvis, a 16-hour documentary that advertised its "all-encompassing" collection of Elvis appearances, used clips from *The Ed Sullivan Show*, *The Steve Allen Show*, and Elvis TV specials. The court thought that these uses went beyond biographical reference and were just rebroadcast as entertainment, often without commentary or interruption. Even though the clips were short – ranging from a few seconds to a minute, many were "the heart" of the original shows, including the moments when Elvis sang his most famous songs.

THE EVER-LENGTHENING COPYRIGHT TERM SEEMS TO BE HAVING THE OPPOSITE EFFECT FROM WHAT THE CONSTITUTION INTENDED...

1998   2018   2038   2078   ?

IT HINDERS ARTISTS WHO WANT TO USE OLDER WORKS, EVEN WHEN THE COPYRIGHT OWNER CAN'T BE FOUND OR WOULDN'T CARE.

THE LONGER TERM ALSO PUTS MORE PRESSURE ON "FAIR USE."

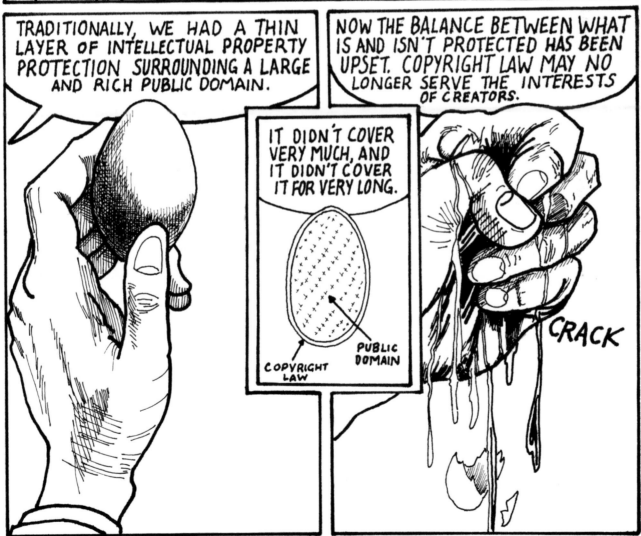

TRADITIONALLY, WE HAD A THIN LAYER OF INTELLECTUAL PROPERTY PROTECTION SURROUNDING A LARGE AND RICH PUBLIC DOMAIN.

NOW THE BALANCE BETWEEN WHAT IS AND ISN'T PROTECTED HAS BEEN UPSET. COPYRIGHT LAW MAY NO LONGER SERVE THE INTERESTS OF CREATORS.

IT DIDN'T COVER VERY MUCH, AND IT DIDN'T COVER IT FOR VERY LONG.

PUBLIC DOMAIN

COPYRIGHT LAW

CRACK

46

48

EVEN IN FEATURE FILMS, THE USE OF TRADE MARKS TO DEPICT "REALITY" HAS BEEN PROTECTED BY COURTS.

CATERPILLAR SUED DISNEY CLAIMING THAT "GEORGE OF THE JUNGLE 2" INFRINGED ITS TRADE MARKS.

HA! HA! HAHA!!

CAT

THE COURT SAID:

IN THE FILM, THE EVIL INDUSTRIALIST TRIES TO DESTROY GEORGE'S JUNGLE WITH "CATERPILLAR" BULLDOZERS. A FEDERAL COURT REFUSED TO BLOCK THE FILM'S RELEASE.

"THE APPEARANCE OF PRODUCTS BEARING WELL KNOWN TRADE MARKS IN CINEMA AND TELEVISION IS A COMMON PHENOMENON."

WHAT ABOUT GETTING PERMISSION FROM PEOPLE WHO APPEAR IN THE DOCUMENTARY?

PERMISSION IS NORMALLY REQUIRED -- PRIVACY IS A LEGITIMATE CLAIM.

WHAZZUP?

CONSIDER FILMMAKER MICHAEL MOORE...

BUT THERE IS AN IMPORTANT FIRST AMENDMENT EXCEPTION THAT LETS YOU SHOW PEOPLE INVOLVED IN MATTERS OF PUBLIC INTEREST, WITHOUT PERMISSION.

MICHAEL MOORE INTERVIEWED JAMES NICHOLS, BROTHER OF TERRY NICHOLS, IN THE DOCUMENTARY "BOWLING FOR COLUMBINE." MOORE SUGGESTED THAT NICHOLS MIGHT HAVE SOME CONNECTION TO THE OKLAHOMA CITY BOMBING ("The Feds didn't have the goods on James, so the charges were dropped.") NICHOLS SUED, CLAIMING MOORE HAD DEFAMED HIM, BUT HE ALSO SAID THAT HIS "RIGHT OF PUBLICITY" HAD BEEN VIOLATED. THE COURT HELD THAT BECAUSE THE FILM ADDRESSED A MATTER OF IMPORTANT PUBLIC CONCERN -- VIOLENCE IN AMERICA -- AND NICHOLS WAS PART OF THE BOMBING STORY, MOORE'S USE OF NICHOLS WAS SPEECH PROTECTED BY THE FIRST AMENDMENT.

DUDE, WHERE'S MY LAWSUIT?

EVEN WHEN THE DOCUMENTARY ISN'T ABOUT SUCH CONTROVERSIAL ISSUES, SOME STATE LAWS ALLOW THE FILMMAKER TO USE A PERSON'S PICTURE WITHOUT PERMISSION IF THE SUBJECT IS "NEWS" OR "PUBLIC AFFAIRS." AND "PUBLIC AFFAIRS" CAN BE DEFINED PRETTY BROADLY.

A DOCUMENTARY ABOUT THE EARLY DAYS OF MALIBU USED SOME FOOTAGE OF FAMOUS SURFER MICKEY DORA, WHO SUED FOR UNAUTHORIZED USE OF HIS IMAGE.

THE CALIFORNIA LAW HAD AN EXCEPTION FOR PUBLIC AFFAIRS AND THE JUDGE SAID A SURFING DOCUMENTARY QUALIFIED.

TO SAY NOTHING ABOUT CREATING AN INTERGALACTIC SUPERHERO!!

"[SURFING] HAS CREATED A LIFESTYLE THAT INFLUENCES SPEECH, BEHAVIOR, DRESS, AND ENTERTAINMENT, AMONG OTHER THINGS."

SO, AS LONG AS I UNDERSTAND THE LIMITS OF THE LAW, I'M SET, RIGHT?

YOU'VE HEARD OF ERRORS AND OMISSIONS INSURANCE?

YES, E&O INSURANCE.

WELL, REGARDLESS OF WHAT THE LAW SAYS, RIGHTS CLEARANCES MAY PLAY OUT DIFFERENTLY IN PRACTICE...

HBO

INSURANCE COMPANIES, UNDERSTANDABLY RISK AVERSE, TYPICALLY REQUIRE A DETAILED LIST OF THE SOURCE AND LICENSING STATUS OF THE MATERIAL IN THE FILM...

TO SHOW YOUR FILM TO A BROADER PUBLIC THROUGH CONVENTIONAL DISTRIBUTION CHANNELS - LIKE HBO OR PBS - YOU NEED E&O INSURANCE TO COVER POSSIBLE LAWSUITS.

SO, WHAT I CAN AND CANNOT USE DEPENDS ON WHAT THE BROADCASTER, DISTRIBUTOR, INSURANCE COMPANY, BROKERS AND LAWYERS ARE COMFORTABLE WITH?

AND BECAUSE THEY GENERALLY DON'T ACKNOWLEDGE "FAIR USE" CLAIMS, THEY MAY REQUIRE CLEARANCES WELL BEYOND THOSE REQUIRED BY THE LAW.

FAIR USES MAY HAVE TO BE CLEARED BY AN ARMY OF LAWYERS OR **CUT** FROM THE FILM?

...BUT I WOULDN'T EXPECT PAYMENT IF MY DOCUMENTARY WAS PLAYING IN THE BACKGROUND OF ANOTHER SHOT!

IF THE GOAL OF COPYRIGHT IS TO ENCOURAGE PEOPLE TO CREATE, THEN THESE KINDS OF RIGHTS CLEARANCES DON'T MAKE ANY SENSE...

IS ANYONE BETTER OFF WITH ALL THESE PAYMENTS FOR TINY FRAGMENTS OF CULTURE?

IS THE IDEA THAT ARTISTS WON'T MAKE FILMS OR MUSIC, UNLESS THEY HAVE THE RIGHT TO CONTROL A FEW SECONDS IN A DOCUMENTARY?

ALL OF THIS INFORMATION HAS BEEN REALLY USEFUL. WHEN I'M DEALING WITH RIGHTS CLEARANCE ISSUES, I'LL HAVE A MUCH BETTER IDEA OF WHAT'S GOING ON.

AND WE'VE ONLY BEEN DISCUSSING WHAT THE LAW AND PRACTICES CURRENTLY ARE ···· **ONE** REASON THEY'RE THIS WAY IS BECAUSE PEOPLE ASSUME THAT'S WHAT ARTISTS WANT. BUT THE LAW AND THE "RIGHTS" CULTURE **CAN** CHANGE IF ENOUGH ARTISTS ARE UNHAPPY WITH THEM!

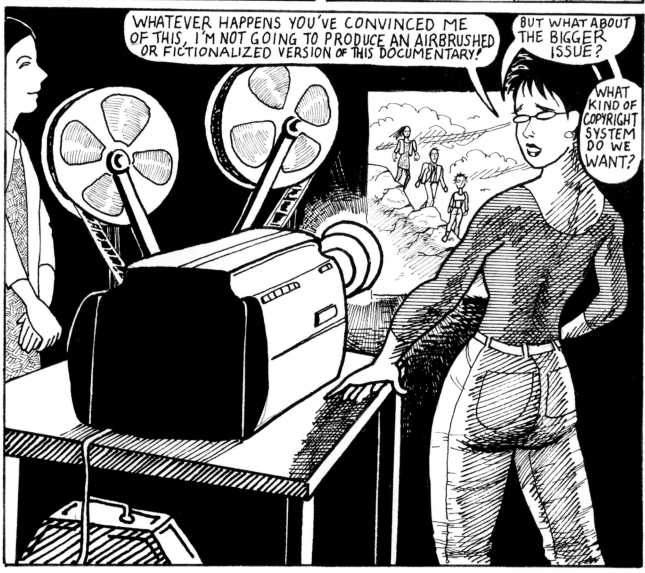

WHATEVER HAPPENS YOU'VE CONVINCED ME OF THIS, I'M NOT GOING TO PRODUCE AN AIRBRUSHED OR FICTIONALIZED VERSION OF THIS DOCUMENTARY!

BUT WHAT ABOUT THE BIGGER ISSUE?

WHAT KIND OF COPYRIGHT SYSTEM DO WE WANT?

THESE SHADOWS HAVE DANCED FOR YOU FOR A FRAGMENT OF TIME.

PERHAPS SOMETHING IN THEIR WORDS HAS CAUGHT YOUR ATTENTION, TAUGHT YOU SOMETHING, GIVEN YOU AN IDEA?

A YOUNG PERSON'S GUIDE TO INTELLECTUAL PROPERTY

BUT NOW THEIR MOMENT IN THE LIGHT IS OVER.

A YOUNG PERSON'S GUIDE TO

UNTIL THE NEXT TIME WE MEET, ALL THAT IS LEFT IS...

NOT YET...

WAIT...

SILENCE.

Afterword

The True Story of *Bound By Law*:
(or 'Why Three Stodgy Academics Wrote a Comic Book')
James Boyle

The authors of this book are frequent, and for the most part, appreciative users of the law of copyright. Keith trained as an artist, has published several comic books and many scholarly articles, and is the bass player for The Garden Weasels – a band that is generally described as being "pretty good considering it is made up entirely of law professors." Apart from her academic work, Jennifer is also a pianist, filmmaker and short story writer. James has written books and numerous articles, and is a columnist for the *Financial Times* online. He also serves on the Board of Creative Commons, a non-profit organization that provides simplified copyright tools for artists and creators. We have all authored copyrighted works, cashed royalty checks, and benefitted from the ability to make "fair use" of copyrighted material in our own creations, whether artistic or scholarly. And we are all also scholars and teachers of copyright law – studying its history, its goals, its constitutional basis, and its impact on the arts. In the process, we have come to admire the way that copyright law has adapted to new media and new technologies through history, maintaining its balance between the realm of ownership and the realm of the public domain – where material is free for all to use without permission or fee. So count us as stodgy believers in the copyright system, not revolutionaries eager to scrap the whole thing.

But from the depths of our stodginess comes this little message – the system appears to have gone astray, to have lost sight of its original goal. Does anyone believe that "the progress of science and the useful arts" is furthered by requiring documentary filmmakers to clear every fragment of copyrighted material caught in their films – even a copyrighted ring-tone on a phone, or a fleeting fragment of TV in the background of a shot? To be fair, in many – perhaps most – cases these demands for payment or clearance have nothing to do with copyright law as it stands. Instead, they are a

manifestation of a "permissions culture" premised on the belief that copyright gives its owners the right to demand payment for *every* type of usage, no matter its length, or its purpose, or the context in which it is set. But that is not, and never has been the law. Copyright may also be adjusting poorly to a world in which everyone can have their own digital printing press; the citizen publishers of cyberspace, the young digital artists, filmmakers and musicians, are unlikely to have high-priced lawyers advising them. The flourishing of digital media has been seen by policymakers mainly as a threat

– as the rise of a "pirate culture of lawlessness." That threat is real. But what is missing is a sense of the corresponding opportunity.

Copyright is not an end in itself. It is a tool to promote the creation and distribution of knowledge and culture. What could be a better manifestation of this goal than a world in which there are few barriers to entry, where a blog can break a major political scandal, a $218 digital film can go to the Cannes Film Festival, a podcast can reach tens of thousands of listeners, a mash-up can savagely criticize the government's response to a hurricane, where recording and remixing technology better than anything Phil Spector ever had may come bundled free with your laptop? Yet for many of these new digital creators, copyright appears more

as an obstacle than as an aid. Sometimes – as with many of the examples we described in this comic book – that may be the result of simple misinformation, a culture of fear and legal threats, or private gatekeepers using copyright law as an excuse to impose deals on artists who lack the information and power to protest. At other times, it seems the law genuinely has lost its internal balance and needs to be reformed – one example might be the extraordinary retrospective lengthening of the copyright term. Just as the digital revolution allows us to offer cheap access to the texts, movies, music and images of the twentieth century, we have extended the length of copyright terms so that most of those cultural artifacts are off limits, even though they are commercially unavailable and their authors cannot be found. But if copyright has sometimes failed, or been applied so that it fails, the answer is not to ignore it, to lose respect for it, to violate it.

One of the under-appreciated tragedies of the permissions culture is that many young artists only experience copyright as an impediment, a source of incomprehensible demands for payment, cease and desist letters, and legal transaction costs. Technology allows them to mix, to combine, to create collages. They see law as merely an obstacle. This is a shame because copyright can be a valuable tool for artists and creators of all kinds – even for many of those who are trying to share their work without charge. Copyright can work in the culture of mash-ups, parodies and remixes, of hypertext links and online educational materials. But it can do so only if we do not let the system slide further out of balance.

We thought about how to present these messages to an audience of artists and filmmakers, how to pass on the information that they need to make the system work for them. But at the same time we wanted to reach a wider audience – an audience of citizens and policymakers who generally hear nothing about copyright except the drumbeat of "Piracy! Piracy! Piracy!" The story of documentary film is vitally important in its own right. Documentaries are the most vivid visual record of our history, our controversies and our culture. But their story is also a manifestation of a wider problem and one that we thought could enrich the public debate on the subject.

For some strange reason, none of our intended audiences seem eager to read scholarly law review articles. What's more, there is something perverse about explaining an essentially visual and frequently surreal reality in gray, lawyerly prose. Finally, what could better illustrate the process we describe than a work which has to feature literally hundreds of copyrighted works in order to tell its story, a living exercise in fair use? Hence this book. It is the first in a series from Duke's Center for the Study of the Public Domain dealing with the effects of intellectual property on art and culture. We hope you enjoy it. For those who are interested in the wider debate on the ownership and control of science and knowledge, or the ideas behind "cultural environmentalism," links to other resources are given on the next page.

Center for the Study of the Public Domain
Duke Law School http://www.law.duke.edu/cspd
"The mission of the Center is to promote research and scholarship on the contributions of the public domain to speech, culture, science and innovation, to promote debate about the balance needed in our intellectual property system and to translate academic research into public policy solutions." An online version of this work is available for free at our website.

Further Reading on Intellectual Property and Culture
James Boyle, The Second Enclosure Movement & the Construction of the Public Domain
http://www.law.duke.edu/pd/papers/boyle.pdf
"It may sound paradoxical, but in a very real sense protection of the commons was one of the fundamental goals of intellectual property law. In the new vision of intellectual property, however, property should be extended everywhere - more is better. Expanding patentable and copyrightable subject matter, lengthening the copyright term, giving legal protection to 'digital barbed wire' even if it is used in part to protect against fair use: Each of these can be understood as a vote of no-confidence in the productive powers of the commons...."

Collected Papers on the Public Domain (Duke: L&CP 2003)
http://www.law.duke.edu/journals/lcp/indexpd.htm
"What does the public domain do? What is its importance, its history, its role in science, art, and in the building of the Internet? How is the public domain similar to and different from the idea of a commons? Is it constitutionally protected, or required by the norms of free expression? This edited collection, the first to focus on the public domain, seeks to answer those questions. Its topics range across a broad swath of innovation and creativity, from science and the Internet to music and culture jamming. Its list of authors includes prominent environmental scholars, appropriation artists, legal theorists, historians and literary critics."

Lawrence Lessig, Free Culture (The Penguin Press, New York 2004)
"A technology has given us a new freedom. Slowly, some begin to understand that this freedom need not mean anarchy. We can carry a free culture into the twenty-first century, without artists losing and without the potential of digital technology being destroyed.... Common sense must revolt. It must act to free culture. Soon, if this potential is ever to be realized."

A Sampling of Legal Resources: **These are not a substitute for legal advice.** For specific legal questions please consult a lawyer.

- **Center for Social Media at American University: Best Practices in Fair Use**
  http://www.centerforsocialmedia.org/fairuse.htm "Documentary filmmakers have created, through their professional associations, a clear, easy to understand statement of fair and reasonable approaches to fair use."
- **Chart on Rights Clearance Problems and Possible Solutions**
  http://www.law.duke.edu/cspd/pdf/docfilmchart.pdf
- **Copyright Overview** http://www.law.cornell.edu/wex/index.php/Copyright
- **The Copyright Act: 17 U.S.C. §§ 101-1332**
  http://www.law.cornell.edu/uscode/html/uscode17/usc_sup_01_17.html
- **Copyright and Fair Use** http://fairuse.stanford.edu
- **Copyright Term and the Public Domain**
  http://www.copyright.cornell.edu/training/Hirtle_Public_Domain.htm
- **United States Copyright Office** http://www.copyright.gov

Selected Organizations
- **Center for the Study of the Public Domain** http://www.law.duke.edu/cspd
  The home of the Arts Project that brought you this comic.
- **Center for Social Media** http://www.centerforsocialmedia.org
  The home of the Best Practices Statement.

- **Chilling Effects Clearinghouse** http://www.chillingeffects.org
  Chilling Effects aims to help Internet users understand the protections that the First Amendment and intellectual property laws give to online activities, with a particular focus on cease and desist letters.
- **Creative Commons** http://creativecommons.org
  Creative Commons builds upon the "all rights reserved" of traditional copyright to create a voluntary "some rights reserved" copyright. It is a nonprofit and all of the tools are free.
- **Electronic Frontier Foundation** http://www.eff.org
  The premier online civil liberties organization.
- **Full Frame Documentary Film Festival** http://www.fullframefest.org/main.html
  The leading documentary film festival in the United States. Takes place each spring in Durham, North Carolina.
- **Motion Picture Association of America** http://www.mpaa.org
  Founded in 1922, the MPAA is the trade association of the American film, video and television industry.
- **Public Knowledge** http://www.publicknowledge.org
  Representing the public interest in intellectual property policy.
- **Volunteer Lawyers for the Arts** http://www.vlany.org
  VLA provides *pro bono* legal services, and educational programs, to the arts community in New York and beyond.

ACKNOWLEDGMENTS

Bound By Law grew out of a conference on the effects of intellectual property law on music and film, which was held in conjunction with the Full Frame Documentary Film Festival. Both the conference and the production and distribution of this book were made possible by a grant from the Rockefeller Foundation. Other support was also provided by the Center for the Study of the Public Domain and by the Office of the President, Duke University.

Debts of gratitude are owed to many people: At Duke, to Garrett Levin, David Lange, Richard Riddell, Eileen Wojciechowski, Jordi Weinstock, Wayne Miller, Nick Drury, Jennifer Carpenter, Scott Lenger and Hiroki Nishiyama. In the filmmaking community Chris Hegedus, Orlando Bagwell and Davis Guggenheim gave us vital material while John Sloss offered a unique legal perspective. Laurie Racine and Joan Shigekawa offered vital support. Peter Jaszi and Pat Aufderheide's work on fair use was invaluable. Larry Lessig's work provided the impetus to focus on documentary film and his scholarship is a vital resource in outlining problems in the area. Along the way, others supplied key encouragement or advice. Thanks to Cory Doctorow, Sham B., Brandt Goldstein, Megan Taylor, the people at Full Frame, and everyone else who made this project possible. Mona Aoki deserves special mention for patience verging on the saintly.

About the Authors

This book was written by James Boyle and Jennifer Jenkins, designed by all of its authors in innumerable, hilarious and occasionally manic conference calls, and drawn by Keith Aoki, a person who (in the opinion of his co-authors) is far too talented to be a law professor.

Keith Aoki is a longtime cartoonist who loves the late 1960s comic work of Jack Kirby, Steve Ditko, Jim Steranko and earlier greats like Will Eisner, Chester Gould and Al Capp. He has also been influenced by the vibrant contemporary work of Robert Crumb, Scott McCloud, Art Spiegelman and Jamie Hernandez. In the mid-1980s, Aoki decided to leave the bohemian art demimonde to go to Harvard Law School. He is now the Philip H. Knight Professor of Law at the University of Oregon School of Law, where he has taught since 1993 and specializes in the area of intellectual property. He has published law review articles in the Stanford, California, Iowa and Boston College Law Reviews and is author of the forthcoming book *Seed Wars: Cases and Materials on Intellectual Property and Plant Genetic Resources.*

James Boyle is the William Neal Reynolds Professor of Law at Duke Law School and one of the founders of the Center for the Study of the Public Domain. He is a Board Member of Creative Commons, and a columnist for the online *Financial Times.* Boyle was the winner of the 2003 World Technology Award for Law for his work on the "intellectual ecology" of the public domain, and on the "second enclosure movement" that threatens it. He is the author of *Shamans, Software and Spleens: Law and the Construction of the Information Society* as well as a depressingly large number of law review articles, and is the special editor of *Collected Papers on the Public Domain.*

Jennifer Jenkins is Director of Duke's Center for the Study of the Public Domain, where she heads its "Arts Project" and teaches a seminar on Intellectual Property, the Public Domain and Free Speech. As a lawyer, she was a member of the team that defended the copyright infringement suit against the publisher of the novel "The Wind Done Gone" (a parodic rejoinder to "Gone With the Wind"). As an artist, she co-authored "Nuestra Hernandez," a fictional documentary addressing copyright and appropriation, and has authored several short stories, one of which was published in Duke's Tobacco Road literary magazine.

Inquiries about the book? Send press, book review, and other inquiries to: cspd@law.duke.edu .

Bulk orders? Educational and other bulk users can order 25 or more copies for classes or conferences at a discounted rate. See www.law.duke.edu/cspd/comics for more information on placing bulk orders.

What's next? Keep up with the activities of the Center for the Study of the Public Domain, including our next comic book on intellectual property and music, by visiting www.law.duke.edu/cspd .

The Center for the Study of the Public Domain is a non-profit organization.